A Memoir of
Who I Was Not

Velma Wilson

Limits of Liability and Disclaimer of Warranty

Printed in the United States of America

ISBN 978-1-941749-27-2

4-P Publishing
Chattanooga, TN 37411

Cover Design by Vanessa Flakes
Editors: Lynn Howard & Dean Arnold

Acknowledgements

There are so many people I need to thank. I want to thank God for allowing me to be in such a beautiful family. To my sister, Dornita, again, I say thanks.

Thanks to my friends for loving on me throughout the years.

Thanks to all who suggested I write this book.

Thanks to the pastors that have given me an opportunity to share in your work for the Lord.

Thanks to David Banks, PhD. for the wisdom you have shared with me to know my purpose.

Thanks to all who shared in this journey. Your encouragement, prayers, and suggestions are priceless.

Thanks to the Serious Writers' Accountability and Training (S.W.A.T.) Camp and Coach Laura Brown for helping me get this book out of my head and onto the pages.

Thanks to Jessica Williams for your advice and prayers.

Thanks to you, the reader. I hope you enjoy my first book.

Email me at msvelmawilson@gmail.com to give me your reviews and feedback!

DEDICATION

**This book is dedicated
To my family**

To My Brothers and Sisters

I am so thankful to be part of a amazing family. I could not have chosen more fantastic, fun and loving brothers and sisters. Thank you for wonderful memories.

To My Husband

Thank you for understanding the time I needed to write this book. Your encouragement in times when I thought I would not be able to continue is priceless. I Love you.

To My Daughter and Son

I am blessed to be chosen to be your Mom. I cannot imagine what my life would have been like without either of you. Thank you for teaching me how to have fun and relax. I love you guys! May the favor of the Lord continue to be upon both of you.

To My Grandson and Granddaughter

Both of you are beautiful gifts from God. I cherish each day I have with you two. Seek the Lord while you are young, for He has an excellent plan for your lives.

CONTENTS

TRAUMA

A Memoir of Who I Was Not is a book about my life and how I came to be who I was created to be—me.

But who I came to be involved some difficult challenges. It included trauma.

My Mother died in childbirth. I was forcibly prevented from attending her burial. At 15, I was raped. And this trauma led to pregnancy.

Are you struggling with why you are acting a certain way? Does it seem like you cannot pull it together in your Christian walk? Maybe you don't consider yourself a Christian. Perhaps you are just coasting through life seeking the next the new trend to bring you joy.

You may have a loving family and be very successful, yet there is an inward void that keeps you thinking of something you may have missed. You cannot explain it, cannot seem to put your finger on it. However, you know it is there.

Trauma can make us feel inadequate, ashamed, unworthy, and guilty.

HelpGuide.org gives describes trauma as "the sudden death of someone close" and "a humiliating or deeply disappointing experience."

Merriam–Webster Dictionary and Thesaurus defines trauma as "a very difficult or unpleasant experience that causes someone to have mental or emotional problems, usually for a long time."

When I began writing this book, it was not going to be about my childhood traumas. After all, I was beyond that, or so I thought. My first book would be about my life but in a different set of events and circumstances.

However, if you have a personal relationship with Jesus, you already know His thoughts are not your thoughts, and it takes personal time with Him for His Spirit to reveal His plans.

On January 6, 2014, Jesus, the Lover of my soul, revealed in a dream the trauma from which He wanted to set me free. It is my hope it may set others free to be themselves as well.

In Psalms, David points out we are fearfully and wonderfully made. He goes on to inform us our frame was not hidden from God when we were made in the secret place, where we were woven together in the depths of the earth. God's eyes saw our unformed bodies; all of the days ordained for each of us were written in His book before one of them came to be. (NIV-Psalm 139:15-16)

All of the days ordained for us were written in His Book before any of them came to be— trauma included. It took personal time with God to develop the love relationship with Christ that would allow me to recognize all of my ordained days—the good, the bad, and the ugly—He would work for my good.

Have you experienced childhood trauma in your life? Do you often find yourself questioning your identity? For me, I could no longer be what the spinning wheels of yesterday had shaped me into. I could no longer remain conformed to this present world. I learned God has a wonderful plan for my life, and I desired to live out every minute of it.

A Memoir of Who I Was Not was written to set the captive free. I was once held captive by my past. As I began to write about my life, I looked back over the years and realized I had no clue about the significance of my natural birth or the actual meaning of my need to be born again (John 3:35).

It took another birthday for me to ask myself if I had lived a life my Creator was proud of. Had I contributed something of value to the world to make it a better place for my generation and the next? Had I lived to my full potential, or had I just coasted along the way? Why am I here?

As I looked through the telescope to the past, I realized I had lived over half a century. I only wish I could take an eraser and erase all my problems, pains and mistakes and try this thing called living again. However, there is no such eraser.

Many have tried to remake themselves in so many different ways. In the end, it was the words of Jesus, "You must be born again," that they finally heard, ringing true like a bell from eternity. I also heard those words.

Now I have been set free from my childhood traumas. I no longer have to be who I was not. What about you? Isn't it time for you to be set free? Isn't it time for you to become who you were created to be?

Whether you are a Christian or not, I pray my story will be a tool to show you how Jesus' love set me free and can set you free. He illustrated, demonstrated, and communicated His love to me. He set me free from living another day of "who I was not."

This book would not have been written without a dream I had on January 6, 2014. God gets my attention in the most unusual ways. It is my hope the following pages will enlighten you and help you to find love, acceptance, and significance.

MEETING MY LOVER

I could not wait to get out of Wanda's car. That twenty-minute ride from Precept Ministries to my two bedroom housing project apartment seemed endless.

Precept Ministries was not a church; it crossed denominational lines and was established for the sole purpose of equipping the saints for the work of service. They taught the willing how to study the word of God on their own.

Wanda was a big, tall woman who was jolly and loud. She was a new Christian and was thirsty to know more about Jesus. At the time, it had been two years since I suggested she enroll in one of the bible study classes. We worked together, and every Monday evening she would pick me up for our class.

Wanda talked me into setting up an appointment on Tuesday evening to meet with Molly concerning my questions about my own salvation.

That evening, after my appointment, my emotions were tumultuous. I felt love, fear, courage, and peace. I laughed, cried, and felt bewildered. I experienced belief and disbelief all at the same time.

While driving me home, Wanda pestered me with questions about my session with Molly. Her questions came like someone throwing darts to hit the bull's eye.

"What did she tell you? Tell me more. How do you feel now? Didn't I tell you that you would find answers to all your questions?" Wanda went on and on.

I tried to answer her as much as I could. But my mind only thought of one thing. I wanted to be alone with the Lover of my soul, the one who made me feel loved. Instead of enjoying this place of peace, I began to drown in the sea of inadequacy. Thoughts were on what I had to offer to the One who exchanged His life for mine.

There I was: a single parent with two children, no transportation, and living in a housing project. All I had was broken dreams to offer Him. Somehow, I knew deep inside me there was an overwhelming joy waiting to be released. I was thankful to Wanda for ensuring I kept that counseling appointment, but at that moment, I needed to be alone. That night, all I wanted to do was go home.

MY BEGINNING

Who knows what may be good for mortals while they are alive during the brief, pointless days they live? Mortals pass by like a shadow. Who will tell them about their future under the sun?

-Ecclesiastes 6:11

GOD'S WORD® Translation

My inner struggles began long before my first session with Molly. My mother died when I was eleven years old. Like many young children who lose a parent, I often felt unwanted, numb, angry, rejected, and guilty. My childhood and adolescence were filled with unexplainable heartaches and pain. I often lived in one of two extremes—at times self-pity, and other times a people pleaser. Both had a profound effect on who I was and who I was not. Looking back, the duplicity of my life kept me in a constant flux, not knowing where or who I was. I didn't know how to be myself.

My beginning

Momma's egg was released from her ovary. That egg met and aligned with my dad's sperm –thus the fertilization of me. Forty weeks later, changes in the connective tissue of my Momma's cervix caused it to soften, and vaginal discharge began to flow. The membranes in the amniotic sac surrounding me ruptured and a large gush of water announced my arrival. Mamma was rushed to the local county hospital.

At Erlanger Baroness Hospital, those penetrating waves of pain continued to move me down the birth canal. My small head facing her pelvis was on a mission. I imagine Momma screaming in agony as my head led the way through like an airplane preparing to land. More pain would have Momma pushing and bearing down until; finally, the umbilical cord was cut. There was the first tap on the buttocks and a loud cry. March 27, 1956, I had officially arrived. My next destination: 361 Cowart Street, on the south side of Chattanooga, Tennessee.

I was the seventh child of my mother, Johnnie Mae Cornelius Boston Roberson. On the day, I was born, my dad, Albert Green Roberson, was in the state hospital having one of his lungs removed. He had tuberculosis. The pollution was so thick in Chattanooga he was forced to move back to Courtland, Alabama.

Momma and her brood of children did not move with him.

Yesteryear, Chattanooga was no different than any other city in the South. Jim Crow was the law of the land for blacks, and racial segregation was a normal way of life. Coloreds or Negroes, as we were called, had to use separate water fountains and bathrooms. South Chattanooga was one of the "negro places." It was where we lived, worked, and played.

At the time, the houses in South Chattanooga were so small you could literally stand at the front door and see all the way through the house to the back door—no more than twelve or so feet wide, sometimes called a shotgun house. There were also magnificent older homes needing major renovations.

Our first house on Mitchell Avenue was a three-bedroom house that needed major repairs. My older brothers had the chore of getting wood and coal to make a fire to keep us warm. There never seemed to be enough wood or coal to last for the week, and many days we were cold. Eating a full course meal at home was a luxury. Most days, we only had beans and cornbread. We ate a lot of beans, Pinto, Navy, Lima – you name it! If it was a bean, we ate it. Breakfast consisted of hoecakes with grits or toast, oatmeal, cream of wheat, or Popeye cereal. We were often hungry.

However, we looked forward to Sundays because that was when we had meat with our meal. Holiday times were even better because we had a traditional holiday meal.

I was at Aunt Minnie's house most of the time. Aunt Minnie was like most of the black women at that time that raised their neighbor's children while those mothers went to work.

She and her husband, Mr. Lewis, kept me on the weekends and during the summers because the old house on Mitchell Avenue was far too small for all of us. Momma and my brother, Cary, who was mentally challenged, shared a bedroom, the boys shared a bedroom, and the girls shared a bedroom.

Aunt Minnie was a very sweet lady. She did not have any children. Mr. Lewis did not allow her to work. He was a very mean man. I would be an adult before I learned she was really my step-grandmother, and Mr. Lewis was my grandfather, my mother's father.

By the time I was four, we had moved to 1608 Mitchell Avenue. I loved that big, aged house. It was pink and white with a big, wrap-around, front porch and a huge bay window. I loved to sit and play on that porch with my doll while Momma combed my older sisters' hair. At night, we were also allowed to stay out later if we stayed on the porch. Although the neighborhood was in need of renewal, it was a good place to raise children.

The pink YMCA was located down the street from our house. It was the beacon of the neighborhood, yet that was one of the places we were not allowed to go. It was for white people. There were still a few whites who lived on Mitchell Avenue. My older brothers and sisters were their playmates.

Momma had an excellent work ethic. She believed in working and taking care of her family. She would sell homemade dinners to make ends meet. Once, she worked as a housekeeper for a white lady who was on welfare. Another time, she was the cook at a local café on Main Street. Since the café was next to the local market, it was convenient for Momma to shop for the fresh meat and vegetables she would cook for lunch. One of my brothers told me she loved working there. However, she was fired for blowing the whistle on her boss. The owner of the café had stolen checks from the White Star Market. She sent Momma to the bank to cash the checks weekly and then had her shop at the very place from where the checks had been stolen. Momma found out what had been going on. She told her boss she had to inform the owner of the market. Her boss fired her on the spot. But being fired did not stop Momma from telling the truth. Her boss was convicted, sentenced, and the café was closed.

When I was six years old, two wonderful things happened in my life. I enrolled in school, and we moved to Maurice Poss Homes, a new 188 unit housing development. Maurice Poss Homes was new and exciting. In addition to a new home, two more brothers were added to the family—a total of nine children in all. There were five bedrooms for all nine of us. For the first time, we did not have to burn wood or coal anymore. We thought we had "moved on up."

We had play clothes, school clothes, and church clothes. That sounds like a lot, but my older brothers and sisters shared clothes. I also remember we had chores, especially on Saturdays. We would all work together to clean the house from top to bottom. Memories of taking every dish, glass, cup, pot, pan, and piece of silverware out of the kitchen cabinets and drawers each week and washing them all (whether we had used them or not) are written upon the tablets of my mind. We washed every cabinet, window, and wall. If it was a part of the inside of the house, it was cleaned, swept, mopped, and wiped down. As a child, I always thought Saturdays were for cleaning, cleaning, and more cleaning.

I attended Howard Elementary School. The Howard School, the first public school in Chattanooga for blacks, was as big as a city block, including an elementary, junior high, and high school. I was so excited to attend. I was not scared because I could walk to school with my big brothers and sisters.

Ms. Smith was my first-grade teacher. She, like other teachers at Howard, was like an extension of my Mother. The Howard teachers not only taught us reading, writing, and arithmetic. They taught us how to behave. And they could whip us.

I was in Ms. Smith'ss class all day. I got to play with other children that did not live in Poss Homes, and some became my new friends.

Two years before my elementary schooling, a group of Howard High School seniors decided to join the movement to the southern states with their own non-violent protests. They planned and staged a sit-in at the lunch counters in two of Chattanooga's downtown five-and-dime stores, Woolworths and S. H. Kress. These stores were places where Negroes could not eat. It was during the time of these sit-ins fire hoses were used on the blacks to discourage equality of the race.

Chattanooga was the first city to use the fire hose on blacks. It would be years later before I understood the bravery of what those students did and how it helped make my environment a better place. At that time, we had a sense they had done something important. Moreover, it helped us to understand that we did not need to be stuck behind the invisible color line, a boundary no one ever talked about.

At school, I was like most children growing up in Poss Homes. Most of us lived in the housing projects or on the surrounding streets such as Cowart, William, Long, Read, and Mitchell. We all went to Howard Elementary. We all stayed on "our side" of Chattanooga. The color line was drawn long before we ever knew what a color line was. Silent rules often speak louder than words. Poss Homes allowed us to keep those voices down by the sense of community we had there. We could not have picked a better place to belong than Poss Homes. Mothers looked out for each other and for each other's children, and we youngsters played well together.

I remember playing with marbles, the bolo paddle, and jacks. Jacks were my favorite. That little rubber ball and the little metal stars kept us entertained for hours. We girls were serious when we played jacks. We would bounce the ball, pick up the jacks, and then catch the ball before it bounced for a second time. It was intense as we swept up our onesies, twosies, threesies, and so forth, until a winner was declared when a player picked up all ten without the ball bouncing the second time or dropping a jack. We could play for hours.

Howard School was not only a place for our education; it also became our recreation outlet as well. There were plenty of things for us to do outside. While the boys played football, baseball, and basketball, the girls played hopscotch, volleyball, and dodgeball. This kept most of us out of trouble. We also had the recreation center by the school football field where I learned how to play ping pong and other table games.

The most exciting time was in the summer when the Howard Marching 100 Band had practice. People came from all areas of the Southside—Alton Park, Westside, Jefferson Street, and sometimes even further, just to see the band perform as they practiced for the upcoming football games. We would make sure we finished our chores and completed our homework so we could go to the field and watch the band practice.

The Howard Marching 100 indeed performed for us. The head drum major would lead the other two or three drum majors, the dancing majorettes, the brass, woodwinds, and percussion instrument players in a series of formations. When it was time for the choreography by all drum majors, we would jump to our feet and without hesitation stand in awe. Some even tried to imitate them. After we had danced and clapped, we would run alongside as they marched off the field. What was even more thrilling was when they would come and march through Poss Homes as they practiced marching in parades. Those memories are priceless.

Momma loved God. She made sure we all went to church at Alleyne Memorial AME Zion Church located on Williams Street. I loved going to church too. One of my special early memories was sipping tea in the downstairs dining area of that church. We would have special "Tea Programs." The tables would be draped in white linen tablecloths and set with little sandwiches, delicate china cups, saucers, and silver teapots. It was so different from home where we would always eat fast so we could get a second serving—if anything was left. Tea etiquette was such a pleasant change of pace. I also loved the people, the songs, and the sermons about how much Jesus loved us.

To me, life at church seemed to line up with the TV program, *The Flying Nun*. Sister Bertrille could fix any problem that came along. She could catch a breeze in that big headgear all the nuns wore. She probably did not even weigh 110 pounds, so if she held her head just the right way the high winds on the coast would lift her up. As a young girl, I wanted to be just like *The Flying Nun* when I grew up. Momma encouraged this desire when she would read Bible stories to us. Watching Momma live her beliefs had a significant impact on my faith in God. I had little understanding of all the religious rituals, but I knew He loved me and I belonged to Him.

My Momma was an excellent mother. She kept us neat and clean. She was firm in her discipline, yet gentle with her hugs. Sunday was my favorite day of the week. I loved to see her dress for church. Her shoes and hats were always the right accessories for the dress or skirt suit she wore. She made sure we looked very nice as well.

I was the youngest girl, so I had two or three dresses of my own I wore on Sundays. She taught us that even if you are poor, nobody had to know it by the way you looked. Being poor was not something I would fully understand until late

ALABAMA

My siblings and I spent summers in Courtland, Alabama with Dad. He lived with our Grandparents, Momma Lesli, and Mr. Ed. We helped our Grandmother with the care of the Kelona Farm. Kelona Farm was once a slave plantation. Now, it is on the registry of historic homes. One of my sisters told me when we were children we would visit Kelona Farm in stages. Boys went first, then the girls. I was eight years old when I could finally go with the others. Momma Lesli and Mr. Ed lived on the farm in the smaller house (as it was called back in the day). In contrast, the big house was the beautiful home of the owner, Ms. Karen. It sat on approximately ten acres. It had four bedrooms, three-and-a-half indoor bathrooms, a library, kitchen, living room, and dining room. Momma Lesli cleaned these rooms daily. She also was the cook. She would cook and clean all day at the big house.

Mr. Ed would tend the fields and the animals. Dad was a foreman on another farm. We worked the farm and had chores. We picked rows and rows of peas, corn, collard and turnip greens, pole beans, tomatoes, and many other vegetables. Then, we washed and prepared them for the freezer. I learned how to milk a cow, churn butter, and even pick cotton. When we were not doing farm chores, there were chores at the house such as ironing linens, pillowcases, and clothes.

On the weekends, Saturday was the day when the black community came together at the only school for blacks. The gym was used for indoor games, and there was always a baseball game. Afterward, the older siblings were able to go to house parties or a club. There they danced to music and enjoyed time away from work. I played house or hide-and-seek with my cousins.

Courtland, Alabama was pure country to city kids like us. The country sun was scorching—hot, humid, and unbearable. But it could not compare with the darkness of the night. There were no outdoor lights, and I do not remember if there was even light from the stars and moon. I can only remember how scared I was to be outside when darkness came. The country darkness made it seem like there had never been light in that area. Some nights it was so dark I did not think the sun would shine in the morning.

Although the darkness was a mystery for me, the thing I despised the most was using the outhouse. I was accustomed to an indoor bathroom back in Chattanooga. Ms. Karen had indoor plumbing, but we were not allowed to use it, and the small house did not have the great comfort of an indoor toilet.

The wooden, rectangular outhouse was some distance from the little house as this helped to minimize the smell. In the darkness of the night, we would use a flashlight to light our way, but it was just miserable. There we were—city kids, trying to use the bathroom while holding the flashlight, inhaling the smell, and listening to all the sounds from the outside. There was no toilet paper like back home. We had to use Ms. Karen's old newspapers or pages from catalogs. I really hated using the outhouse in Alabama. I disliked the "piss pot" that was kept in the house just as much. If it was not emptied regularly, the whole house would be filled with an awful odor. We used it only for urinating or when there was inclement weather. Otherwise, to the outhouse we went.

One of my fondest memories of Alabama was Momma Lesli's delicious food. She cooked all the meals for both houses. She did not look at cooking for us as a chore. It was a passion to serve all of us each day. We ate breakfast at the big house. Early in the morning, as we entered the kitchen of the big house, the aroma of country ham, fresh eggs, churned butter, home-made biscuits, and fresh squeezed orange juice would awaken our appetites. At lunch and dinner, three to four-course meals were served in Momma Lesli's smaller home. She would carry the meals from the big house. At the noon table, we would find the table set with crispy fried chicken, mashed potatoes, green beans, and homemade rolls along with a glass of tea. At 6:00 p.m., dinner was served, and we might find fresh garden turnip greens and fried pork chops, or macaroni and cheese and chicken and dressing, or many other delicious dishes.

There was almost always cornbread or homemade rolls. A homemade chocolate cake or fried apple pies made us never want to leave the table. We would eat and eat, indulging our taste buds and satisfying our hunger to the point of over indulging. Without a doubt, Momma Lesli was a great cook, and our stomachs testified to that fact.

When we went in the mornings to the big house, we were not allowed to go past the kitchen. After Ms. Karen was served in her dining room or on the veranda, we would eat breakfast in the kitchen.

Her dog, Susie, ate with us. Literally, the dog ate at the table with us. I am not sure whose chair was next to Susie's. I do know it was degrading. Sometimes, Susie would stay in the chair chowing on a T-bone steak cut up in her bowl. Other times, she would jump out of the chair, and one of us would place her bowl on the floor. We all hated the dog being at the table, but we kept that amongst ourselves.

Henry, Momma Lesli's adopted son, really did not like the way the dog was treated. The dog had her own bed in the big house, and we had to iron her bed linen. The dog was treated far better than Henry. I imagine he hated a lot of things about that farm. He was the first teenager I saw that did not do everything an adult told him. I thought that was strange since I was always taught to obey adults.

One morning as we were all sitting at the table, Henry was in a particularly bad mood. We all did our usual fussing or complaining about the dog being at the table and having his bowl set like the rest of us. Henry told us, one day, he would poison the dog. He had had enough.

It may have been a day or two after he had spoken those words that little Susie was found dead. We did not know whether Henry poisoned her or not. But one thing for sure, we all suspected it. Ms. Karen suspected it as well. She went berserk. She came in the kitchen and threatened each of us if we did not tell who poisoned her furry friend, Susie. There was never a confession.

All of us were forced to attend her pet's funeral. But the next day at the breakfast table we were all smiling quietly. We were sorry Susie was dead; however, it felt great to be at the table without that dog. It was one of those days when I did not complain about anything in Alabama.

Momma Lesli had fourteen brothers and sisters. So, I had lots of uncles, aunts, and cousins. I enjoyed being with my cousins. It seemed like everybody was some kin to each other. If not for the outhouse and mosquitos, I think I would have enjoyed it much more.

In 1967, I expected and hoped to say, like my sisters had, "I can't wait to go back next summer." But that never happened. 1966 was the last time we visited Alabama in the summer as children. Something so tragic happened that Alabama became only a memory we discussed at the dinner table in Chattanooga. This tragedy changed life as I knew it. It marked the end of who I was and the beginning of who I was not.

THE KISS GOODBYE

"A kiss that is never tasted is forever
and ever wasted."

—Billie Holiday

On Saturday, April 22, 1967, my family walked two-by-two down the aisle of Alleyne Memorial AME Zion Church. At the end of the aisle, I walked in with my brothers and sisters, and we stood, with tears in our eyes and screams from our mouths, we looked upon Momma lying in a casket. We were seated in the first pew in the church. The church was filled with other family members and friends. All of us were dressed in our Sunday's best attire, just like Momma would have wanted. She looked so lovely.

Several Pastors sat in a row from one end of the pulpit to the other end. One of them walked to the podium that stood in the center. There was a large choir in the area behind them. I listened a little for a short time as he read the scripture and asked us to bow our heads for prayer. When I closed my eyes, his voice was in the background of the thoughts in my head. I thought about how a few weeks earlier, Mom and the rest of the family celebrated my eleventh birthday. Just last week, she had left to go to the hospital to give birth to her tenth child. She kissed me goodnight and said she would be back in three to four days. She never came back. Tears flowed from the eyes of everyone. In fact, there were so many people screaming and hollering that it all seemed like a dream. I kept thinking I would wake up, and all of this would be over. But it was not a dream. I was eleven years old, and momma was dead. The open casket brought those thoughts to reality.

I kept crying with the rest of my family; however, memories continued to flood my brain.

> *Just last week Momma had sent me to the Five and Dime Store on Main Street to buy some plastic curtains for a bedroom. She gave me the money and told me what color to choose.*

A couple of nights ago she tucked me in bed.

A couple of nights ago she combed my hair in five ponytails for school the next day.

Momma had made a promise to me that I was next in line to have my own bedroom. She trusted me with her money. She always made me look pretty. She told me I would grow up and be someone special. She said I had a kind heart. Momma where are you?

I tried to listen to the Methodist preacher as he delivered her eulogy; however, I could not follow along with anything he said. When the songs, scriptures, and prayers were over, someone got up and closed the casket. Six pallbearers, flower girls, the preacher, and the funeral home staff began the family procession out of the church to the hearse and the shiny black limousine that was parked and waiting for us.

41

Halfway down the aisle, one of my sisters needed help just to walk. Her screams for Momma led to the rest of us calling for her. Seeing other people crying as well ripped at my heart. My tears were part of my own sorrow but seemed a part of theirs as well. As we got ready to get into the family vehicle, my elementary principal whispered in a lady's ear. The woman walked over to my younger brothers and me and told us she was taking us home.

"No," I said. "I want my Momma."

My elementary school principal, said, "Take the younger kids home. I do not think they can handle the grave site service."

"No," I said, "I want to go with my brothers and sisters."

She gave me a stern look as she grabbed both of my hands and turned me around to look directly into her cock -eyes.

"You are going home like I said." She said sternly.

After that, to be truthful, I did not know if I was crying because I lost Momma, because I could not go to the gravesite, or because I was scared of the face that was looking down at me. At that moment, a part of who I was and what I wanted no longer mattered. Do what this woman is telling you to do, I thought. So I got into an unknown lady's car and she took the four of us, the youngest, home.

When we arrived home, there were lots of people there. I had a strange feeling this house would never again be the home I had known. For years to come, I would no longer be the quiet, yet full of life young girl who had wanted to be a teacher or a psychiatrist. Although I was not the one who physically died, something inside of me died that day. I would become a young girl who was unsure of who she was or how she would get through life.

What happens to children when their parents die young? In his article, "Losing a

Parent as a Child," Joana E. Bruno points out that losing a father or mother as a child can be a trauma that is very hard to overcome, especially if the child is very young. It changes the child; it changes her future, her personality, her beliefs, her fears, her cravings, and the way the child perceives the world.

This is certainly what happened in my life. I changed into someone I was not. In fact, Momma's death changed all of us. After Momma's death, I do not remember any adult ever mentioning her again. I think they believed they were protecting us.

My soul cried out for years. I did not recognize the voice or the need. You see, there were silent rules I had obeyed most of my life that were louder than the sweet voices trying to rescue me from the day my principal said I could not go to Momma's grave site.

From that day forward, I had a fear of those in authority. I was as obedient as I could be.

The problem, however, was adults surrounded me. It seemed like one of them was always telling me what I could or could not do. Even my older brothers and sister told me what to do.

I felt I did not have a say so in most things. My right to be a loved and cherished child was vetoed. "You are a motherless child. Someone else has to take care of you. Do not be a problem," I would say to myself.

MY SISTER-PARENT

"I wasn't concerned about the hardships because I always felt I was doing what I had to do, what I wanted to do and what I was destined to do."

—Katherine Durham

Albert Green Roberson was Momma's husband for almost fourteen years. He moved back to Chattanooga after her death. At first, he took care of us very well. We all called him Albert Green. I am not sure if any of us called him Dad. I don't think he was the father of all of us. (I actually don't know, even to this day.) At any rate, he had a way of making us believe anything he promised, and he quickly convinced others to have sympathy for anything he wanted or needed.

One time, I remember going to the bank with him to cash a check. When it was time to transact his business with the teller, he began to cry and share his story of how his wife had died and he had to take care of all these children—pointing down at the three of us who were with him. The cashier gave him his money, and as he walked toward the door, some of the people who were waiting in line gave him money as we passed. In the car, he stopped crying.

His efforts to be a dad to us were short lived. He had dated several women since Momma's death, but there was one woman who shot him with Cupid's arrow. She was a neighbor who had been one of Momma's friends. She lived in the row of houses behind us and had twelve children. It did not take him long to figure out he could not live in two places at the same time. The strain was more than he could bear. So he checked out of our lives.

Life is strange. The parent who had lived at a distance for so long who could not change into being a stay-at-home dad, was still around. But, Momma, who worked hard to take care of her children, died.

When Albert Green moved into the house behind us, the fourth sibling, my sixteen-year-old sister, stepped into the parent role. The oldest sister had married and left home. There were two brothers older than she, and five of us were younger. Our oldest sister was married and not living at home, and the oldest brother was in and out of the house.

The brother who was a senior in high school worked at White Star Grocery and was able to bring home meat from time to time.

Albert Green was getting a social security check for our care. My sister never saw a penny of it.

With Albert Green leaving us alone so early after Momma's death, life was hard. We learned to live in survival mode. Where would the next meal come from? Who has grown out of their clothes? Since I was the youngest girl and very skinny, I could not wear my sister's clothes. I only had a few outfits to wear, over and over. None of us had the time or even knew how to grieve. There were many days we were fed by some of the adults that lived in Poss Homes, and many other days we were just hungry.

By now my sense of normalcy was quickly disappearing. I had a sixteen-year-old sister-parent who did her best to keep our family together. Her name is Dornita, but everyone calls her by her nickname, "Hatchet." After she graduated from high school, she became a parent herself. We had a baby in the house that seemed more like my little sister than my niece. I do not know why my sister was called, "Hatchet." I do know she began to live up to that name. She did not mind chopping you to pieces with her words of authority.

The pressure on my sister-parent was increasing. Hatchet was still under-aged, and she did not want the authorities to find out there was not and adult living in the house. The brother who graduated soon afterward enlisted in the Navy. I remember thinking if I did what I was supposed to do and what I was told to do, maybe I would not go to a foster home. I did all I could to not lose my family and have to live with strangers.

Hatchet had learned from our Mother very well. Momma was an orderly, neat and clean person. We were trying to do everything Momma had done. We cleaned, cleaned and cleaned. Now we added cooking to the list. Hatchet began to teach us how to take care of each other. My sister Judy was the cook at that time. She had learned a lot from Momma Lesli.

Like Momma, my sister had strict rules, and I wanted so much to please her so I would not get into any trouble. Of course, I could not always pull that off. Just being a little girl, I would do something like play instead of washing dishes like I was supposed to do. Sometimes I was not even sure what it meant to please her. How could I please someone who had so much responsibility at such a young age?

Hatchet was an avid reader. Although she read all types of books, Harlequin Romance novels were her favorite. She made sure we read. In fact, when she would ask us questions, and we did not know the answer, we had to read out loud at the foot of her bed while she lay and read her own book. It never occurred to me she wasn't listening but was reading her own book. However, I was so scared of being scolded I would skip most three syllable words as I read aloud. To this day, I have a hard time pronouncing some of them.

My sister was firm like Momma. She made sure we obeyed. Had she not been tough, who knows which one of us, or all of us, would have tried to challenge her. Her goal was to teach us how to take care of ourselves. She made sure we knew we had to finish school. My sister was so smart and spoke with such authority it never occurred to me she was only six years older than me.

Since school was important to Hatchet, school was important to me. I was pretty smart myself, thanks to the home reading assignments. I still had my little girl dreams. Some days I wanted to be a teacher; then, other days a psychologist, a wife, a millionaire, a writer, or even a nun.

I had a quiet spirit but was not shy. I ran for Miss Howard Elementary and won, but my celebration was short lived. My homeroom teacher called me into the office and explained to me that I could not be Miss Howard Elementary. She intended to give it to one of my classmates whose sister had won Miss Howard Junior High. She thought it was the right thing to do since their mother was a teacher. I felt like a nobody. I lived in the projects. My mother had passed, and my dreams no longer mattered. I cried through the rest of the school day. By the time I got home, I had believed I was nobody. I didn't even bother to tell my sister of my "loss." Who I was not was taking shape.

I remember days when the weight of raising us was too much for my sister parent to bear. She had a child of her own, worked in the daytime, and went to the University of Tennessee at Chattanooga, in the evening.

Occasionally, she would tell us she couldn't do this anymore. She would have us all to get in her car and would drive us to the Chambliss Children's home. I would cry all the way. I thought I would never come back. Once inside the Chambliss Home, she would go into an office, and my two brothers and I would sit in the chairs in the hallway outside the office. It was always at night when we went.

I'm not sure if my brothers were as frightened as I was. At set time, the lights would go out, and only very dimmed lights remained on in the hall. A nurse dressed in all white from head to toe would walk down the hallway. The medicine bottles she had in her hand would jiggle next to the metal case she carried. The sound of the bottles and her clacking shoes were frightening to me as she walked down what seemed like a very long hallway. Sometimes when she passed by, she would smile.

Other times she would look straight ahead as if we were not there. I surely did not want to live there. I can't count how many times I vowed to myself to be good if we made it back home.

When it seemed like forever, the office door would open. The Chambliss Home worker would always say the same thing, "I have talked to your sister. She is going to give you all another chance. You all better behave because I told her the next time she could leave you all here." We would all nod our heads and then head to the car for home.

Those visits were some of the scariest days of my life. My brothers often asked me why I cried every time, and they assured me Hatchet was not going to leave us there. Deep in my heart, I knew my sister parent loved us and would not leave us. Yet, because of fear, I could not shake the thought this may be the day when we had gone too far.

My brother Cary was diagnosed with spinal meningitis several months after he was born. Meningitis is an inflammation of the membrane of the brain and spinal cord. This bacterial disease affected his right side and left him mentally challenged. He would have severe seizures often if he did not take his medication. He would sometimes sleep over to Albert Green's house. His bed, we found out, was the bathtub. His food was the leftover scraps from our stepbrothers and stepsisters. Whether he was invited to come over or wandered over there on his own because of his Dad, I will never know. I do know he did not understand the mistreatment he was subjected to. When Hatchet found out about it, she made sure he no longer went to Albert Green's. He was later accepted in Pinewood, a residential facility for the disabled.

Hatchet got a job making pizza. At eighteen, she began working at the Chattanooga Housing Authority. My brother in the Navy would send money home to help out. These funds helped relieve some of the strain of our day-to- day life.

When Hatchet turned twenty-one, she got legal custody of the four of us. She did not have to adopt my sister Judy because she married at seventeen. Hatchet would work at the Housing Authority during the day and attend the University of Tennessee at

Chattanooga in the evenings. So I became the cook at fourteen years old. It was not a job I was thrilled about. I burnt most meals thinking I would give that responsibility to my brother, who was one year younger than me. But burning the food never released me from cooking duties.

By age fifteen, I had a new sense of normalcy. There had not been a tragic event for a while. We had food on our table. I had a summer job and could buy my school clothes. We would watch television together. There was always someone in the neighborhood at our house. We would laugh at jokes or try to dance as we listened to the Motown sounds. It was nice to laugh and not cry. I also had friends in school and by now I could stay longer at my friends' houses as long as their parents were home.

My friends would have parties at their houses. During one of those parties, I was introduced to a young man that liked my friend's sister. I learned he was in my class.

He was very kind and considerate. He lived in Alton Park. For some reason, he talked more with me at the socials. Although we were not dating, he had Hatchet's approval to hang out at our house. He was a trustworthy person.

Hatchet often told us she would not be raising our children. She was raising us, and that was enough. Sex, to me, was out of the question. I did not want to disappoint my sister, so going without dating was not a big deal to me.

WHEN "NO" MEANS "NO"

"In Every Language, No Means No"

—Canadian Federation of Students

The sun was shining, and there was plenty of time to get to the softball field before the game started. I changed my school clothes and completed my chores. I was free to go outside. I stopped along the way to buy a Sprite and some chips at the neighborhood vending truck we called "Thomas Truck." Thomas, the owner, came at least three times a day. His music summoned us to the oasis of candy, pickles, chips, cookies and sodas that our five, ten and twenty-five cents could buy. We knew exactly what time he would be in our section of the housing projects. We would make a dash out of the house, eager to buy our goodies before he moved to the next area of the projects.

While waiting for Mr. Thomas to hand me my goodies, a guy that lived in the neighborhood as well as attended Howard, asked me where I was going when I left Thomas's Truck. After answering his question on where I was going, he told me he was also going to the game but needed to change his school clothes.

"Hey," he said. "Walk home with me. I will change clothes, and we can walk together."

Since we lived in the same neighborhood and knew one another, it being a problem never occurred to me. When we arrived at his house, He asked me to come in as he unlocked the door. I sat on the couch in the living room, and he ran upstairs to change. I picked up a magazine and opened my Sprite and began eating my chips. After he had come down the stairs he locked the door we entered. I thought that was strange but reasoned we would exit another way. He calmed my suspicion when he announced we would leave through the back door.

As we were leaving, he grabbed my arm and asked for a kiss. I said no, and told him I was ready to go. He said he would let me go if I kissed him. Up until this time, I had not kissed a boy. I kissed his cheek and put my hand on the back door knob to leave. He grabbed me and turned me toward him. He kissed me on my mouth, and I told him we needed to leave so we would not miss the start of the game. He did not turn me loose. I struggled for freedom, but after his hold on me, I knew freedom was not coming soon. I fought, we struggled. The more I shouted "No! Stop, don't do this," the more he persisted. My pleas were ignored. What I wanted didn't matter. He managed to pin me on the tile floor with one of my arms bent behind my back. With one hand, he was able to do what I could not stop him from doing. I was afraid and wanted to go home. Tragedy had once again found its way into my life. And there was nothing I could do to prevent it. I felt hopeless. Helpless. I completely shut down.

Afterward, he got up and pulled up his pants. I got up and did the same. Without a word, I unlocked the front door and walked outside. The sun was still shining. I was dejected and broken and wondered what just happened. I asked myself, *"Why did I stop at Thomas Truck? Why did I go with him? Why? Why? Why? How stupid are you?"* These thoughts raced through my head. Confused and dazed I wasn't sure if the softball game had even started. What I did know was this person had made a home run, which should have been an "out." By the time I entered into my house, I had wanted to bathe and vomit at the same time. I was too ashamed to tell anyone. I tried to act as if nothing had happened. I did not want my sister-parent to be suspicious. I kept my same routine. I took on the identity of who I was not created to be.

Remember when I told you one of my little girl dreams was to be the Flying Nun? Well, that dream is impossible now. Two months later, I knew something was wrong and for the first time in my life, I questioned God. Yes, the God my Momma loved and read to us about. The God Hatchet talked about. The God I had learned to love and prayed to. Where was He? I asked Him in anger, "God, are you the God that protects us or not?" "You are the giver of life. Why under this circumstance?" I shouted at God. "Don't you remember? I was supposed to be The Flying Nun!"

After I asked all I could ask, I cried, took a deep breath, and pointed my small finger toward heaven and said, "You are the giver of life, and it will be You, not me, that make this baby live and be someone special."

NOTHING STAYS A SECRET FOREVER

"Confession is always weakness. The grave soul keeps its own secrets and takes its own punishments in silence."

-Dorothy Dix

I remember going to school late every day after my morning sickness. I was still very petite, and there was no sign of me showing what was taking place inside of me. I had not told a soul yet. It is amazing how I was able to act normal when everything about me was abnormal. I began reading Hatchet's Harlequin Romance books in my room.

The classmate I met at my friend's party was still coming around, yet a boyfriend was the furthest thing from my mind. I still kept my usual routine in the evening time. I hung out with friends, went to the movies, or watched the Howard's Marching 100 band.

One September evening, one of my girlfriends and I were on our way to see the band. As we got closer to the Marching 100, she touched my stomach and simultaneously asked me if I was pregnant. Of course, the lie of gaining weight was unbelievable because she had touched my stomach. I could not zip my pants up, and I had on a red sweatshirt with the sleeves cut off so I would not be too hot since it was still warm during those early days of September. I knew then the time had come to tell someone.

There was only one person I could tell. He was the young man that really wanted to be my boyfriend. It was obvious he liked me, so I knew he would be someone I could trust with my fears. The next day in school I told him I needed to talk to him after school. We met on the side of the school where the gymnasium leads to the entrance to the school building.

It was on those stairs I shared what took place on that awful day. He asked me why I waited so long. I replied, telling him how ashamed and scared I had been. I explained how much I wanted to tell; however when I thought I had gained the courage to tell my sister-parent, I would remember what she had told us over and over:

"I am taking care of all of you; I will not be taking care of your children."

That little bit of courage would disappear as quickly as it came.

This young man reminded me how much he liked me, and everyone in our circle of friends knew that as well. He always talked about me with his family and friends. He stated they would probably think he was the baby's father and about how embarrassed he would be. We sat there silent for a couple of minutes.

He broke the silence by suggesting he could say he was the baby's daddy. I thanked him for the offer, but I told him I would tell the truth when the time came. For a few months, I had tried to cover up my dark truth. It had really taken a toll on me. I did not want to add another cover-up to an already messed up situation. He told me he wanted to talk to the young man who did this to me and would let me know if he decided to do that. I walked home realizing I did not have long before everyone else would know.

A couple of days after our meeting, the time to tell Hatchet had come. I was at upstairs, at home and I heard the front open. Hatchet's voice boomed from bottom of the stairs.

"Velma, come down here now!".

I stepped into the living room where she stood. She told me what she had heard from someone who sat next to her on the bus. She shouted "you are pregnant." She was furious, just like I thought she would be. After all, she was not going to raise "our children." The time had come. Truth bells were about to ring. So I began to tell her what happen on that frightful evening. I was covered with shame as I told her my story. Tears began to flow like a river from my eyes.

When the last word left my lips, her immediate response stunned me. She spoke the most unbelievable words I ever heard: "I do not believe you."

She did not believe me. I felt as if someone had thrown a dagger in my heart. She really did not believe me! She said I was covering up for the young man that was always coming around. I explained to her he and I had never kissed, let alone had sex.

She told me to stop talking and call the guy she had trusted to come over. I called him and explained what happened. When he arrived, my sister-parent sent me upstairs so she could talk to him alone. Each step I placed my feet on was like a piano keyboard. The tune was a sound of voices from the past, particularly my elementary school principal's voice, which caused me wither into submissive silence. I walked up the stairs murmuring in a melancholy voice, "Do what this woman is telling you do. My life was not my own."

Upstairs, I thought about all of the times I tried to be good so I would not have to be separated from my family. Now I was going to be put out for something that was not my fault. Waiting for my fate seemed like an eternity.

Finally, my sister-parent stood once again at the foot of the stairs and asked me to come down. When I got there, he was gone. She said he had told her the "truth." I was relieved. She would now know what I had suffered. I would not have to leave home. With a sigh of relief, I went back to my room and went to bed. The next day she made me an appointment at the health center.

My trip to the Alton Park Health Center began with me sitting in the back seat. Hatchet and my aspiring, by default boyfriend were up front. Hatchet told me after the visit with the doctor we were now going to buy maternity clothes. The two of them talked about a name for the baby and more things that required no input from me. They talked as if the baby was his. I was stunned. Listening in the back seat reminded me of the time at the gravesite. *You have no say so in this matter. Just do what this adult is telling you.* The doctor said I was at the end of my fifth month of pregnancy.

The school year began, I was in the eleventh grade and had a boyfriend by default. The boy who always wanted to be my boyfriend became just that. He told everyone the baby was his and even got a second shift job. He still had not gotten a kiss from me and barely got a hug. I did not understand why someone would have such an interest in me or why he was so kind. I was coasting through life. I had other hurdles ahead to jump. Trying to love someone was not one of them.

I was jaded to the reactions of others. One of the ladies that helped my sister-parent from the beginning shook her head when she saw me one day. She told me no one could have told her I was that kind of girl. I did not try to explain. I was not the person she or others thought I was. I was not even the person I knew I was. Such is life in these circumstances.

My second prenatal visit was located on Third Street at the Hamilton County Health Department. I had to go by myself. I had never ridden the city bus alone. I was scared of the people on the bus and even more frightened of the people in the waiting room. This place was crowded with mostly old people. Some were coughing, others moaning in pain.

I had to go up to the front desk. It was taller than I was. The receptionist handed me some papers to fill out and asked that I return them when they were completed. I answered her questions concerning why I was there, then she gave me a number and told me to have a seat. She stamped a form or two, and as she gave them back to me, she explained that when I heard the nurse call my name, I needed to get up and follow her.

She knew I was scared, and her attentive concern eased me for a moment. I sat down next to a lady with a crying baby. I picked up a magazine so I would not have to talk to anyone and so as not to pay attention to the baby, but the baby cried so loud I got up and moved to the other side.

How I wished I had stayed with the crying baby! On the other side, two rows away sat Albert Green and his stepdaughter. I could not believe it. I had to come to this health center by myself, and he was sitting there with His lover's daughter. She, too, was pregnant. She did not have to wait outside in the cold for the bus, all alone. She did not have to sit in a crowded place with strangers. She had someone to drive her and comfort her as she waited until her name was called. She had my Dad.

I wanted to get up and run out the door. Instead, I sat there and allowed self-pity to become my friend. Why do I not have a momma or a dad? Why would God take Momma? Why would he allow such terrible things to happen to me? One thing I was now sure of: there was not a God as I had believed. He no longer existed.

After a couple more visits, it was time for my daughter to arrive. She was born premature and weighed 2lbs 12 ounces. I was able to go home; she stayed. Once home, I had to wait at least six weeks before I could go back outside. The old folks said my "pores," need to close. My baby girl stayed in the hospital for about two and half months. Because of the "six-week" rule imposed by the wisdom of the "old folk", I wasn't allowed to go visit her at the hospital. With that entire time passing coupled with her extended stay, I was beginning to wonder if I actually had given birth or was it just a dream.

However, when I saw her for the first time, I knew then she was my little girl. She had my genes. She was a part of me. She was mine. It did not matter how she got here.

My distorted belief that no one loved me had no bearing on my daughter's need to be loved and cared for. To the best of my warped ability, my motherly instinct went to the extreme. She was beauty out of an ugly circumstance.

NEW BEGINNINGS

Your eyes saw me when I was formless; all my days were written in your book and planned before a single one of them began.

-Psalms 139:16

Holman Christian Standard Bible

Four years later, I had married, divorced, and was a single mother. I married the man who consistently showed me his love. The marriage did not last long. He deserved someone who could respond to love with love. I was not that person. I was not emotionally fit.

He remarried, and I became a single parent. I had a son by the man I was dating. Being a single parent was wonderful for me. I did not take my responsibility lightly. We were poor. The jobs I worked were minimum wage jobs or seasonal jobs. Most of the time I worked two jobs just to make ends meet.

My kids were four years apart. They sparked feelings I had suppressed for a long time. I had learned a lot from my sister parent. I knew how to cook, take care of them and you know I knew how to clean! Although, I had a lot to learn on how to express my love, they made it easy. My daughter and son became my reason for living. It was hard yet normal for me to be a single parent. I was raised without a father or mother. The years growing up with my niece, (Hatchet's daughter,) when I was still young, paid off. I got some practice with her.

While my daughter was submissive, my son was ever the explorer. His personality always gave us a fun-filled adventure. He loved to play. I learned to be playful. We were a family. They fought like brothers and sisters sometimes did.

They both were good children indeed. I raised my children in a time where others help and advice was welcomed. I still believed in doing what others told me. I am thankful the ones I listened to who gave me sound advice. It really did take a village to teach me great lessons on parenthood.

I worked at a factory in Rossville, Georgia. It was there God reintroduced Himself to me.

One of the ladies I worked with was named Freda. She was a godly woman for sure. She was the first person in a long time that caught my attention because she actually lived her Christian faith.

I gave her a hard time. Freda would tell me God loved me. My reply would be, "God is like Santa Claus." I was the spokesperson who spoke against God. God was just stories that people told to children. I was not a child anymore. But Freda never stopped portraying His love to me. No matter how I treated her or what I said, her temperament was the same—gentle, kind, and full of God's love.

At lunch one day, six of us were sitting in the break room eating. One of the ladies at the table told us her husband had been laid off. I asked her how they were going to make it because our own time to be laid off was quickly approaching. (Soon, after Halloween, we were laid off until the next year. It would be the first part of spring before we would be called back to start making costumes again.) She assured me she was not worried. She told me they were praying about it, and God would make a way. I told her she was wasting her time. Her husband needed to go out and find another job.

The strangest thing happened after lunch. I went back to my work area so angry. In the last couple of years, anger had become my ruling emotion. This particular day, it was ruling my heart at the very thought of someone trusting a God I no longer believed worked things out.

That night I had fallen asleep watching television. Sometime between night and morning, I truly had a visit from the Lord. I did not see His face, and I cannot tell you how He looked. What I can tell you is I heard His voice. It was as clear as someone sitting next to me and talking.

He asked me one question: "Why do you keep saying I do not exist?"

That was all. I waited to hear something else, but I did not. I could not shake the question He asked.

One thing I knew to do well was react. My reaction was to reason that maybe there is a God, but He is not for me. Besides, how could He be for me? I knew I was not worthy. I had denied him. I told people God did not exist.

I was filled with condemnation, anger and guilt. I had gone too far. I went even deeper into hopelessness. During this time, I was not living, I was merely existing. I believed even God could not love me now. However, God was not like I thought. I was judging Him by how my earthly father loved me.

In my twenties, a set of unusual circumstances caused me to begin learning how God loves me. I changed babysitters, and my new sitter was a Christian. She would often ask me to go to church. I would tell her I would go, even though I had no intention of going. One Saturday, my regular grocery shopping day, I walked to the neighborhood Red Food Grocery Store. I was within walking distance, as I did not have a car. With my prepared list, I went from one aisle to another looking for an item I could not find. Then I heard someone call my name. It was the babysitter, who also shopped at this grocery store. Interestingly, I had never seen her here before. We hugged and talked about our lists of things to buy, and once again she asked me to go to church. This time she told me she was not taking no for an answer. She would pick me up Sunday, no matter what. I agreed; however, I was not really sure if I would actually go.

That evening, a friend and I went to the local mall. Neither of us had money for shopping, but it gave us something to do. One of the major stores in the mall was remodeling and was very disorganized—they had stuff everywhere. We could not help but notice all the new fall clothes on prominent display. That rack seemed to call our names. We got a couple of outfits and headed to the dressing rooms to dream a little.

The department store had made an area for shoppers to try on clothes next to a big sign that said, "Please excuse our mess, we are under construction." When we arrived in the makeshift dressing area, we could not believe what we saw—white women and black women were stuffing all the garments they could fit into their pocketbooks. The "dressing area" had become a place to take what you wanted for free. My friend and I looked at each other and said, "Why Not?" We took the items we had in our hands and put them in our pocketbooks and left that store in a hurry.

I had never stolen anything before. I did not even know what I had taken until I got home. After going into the house, I crept upstairs to my bedroom like the police were in the house waiting for me. I was so terrified. I closed the door and waited until my heart stopped beating so fast. I opened my pocketbook and looked to see what I had risked my freedom for. The stolen clothes were two skirt sets.

I sat on the bed, disgusted with myself. I do not even wear dresses or skirts. Then a strange thought came to mind. "God, I asked, "do you really want me to go to church? Is this why I have these clothes?" So out of fear—and to ease my conscience of what I did—I went to church that Sunday.

Of course, God did not—I repeat *did not*— approve of me stealing those dresses. However, since I was in His house, He had my attention. The preacher was a sharp dresser and had a way with words I had never heard before. He mixed the scriptures with everyday life.

According to his preaching, everything I was doing was wrong. Remember, I claimed God was for others but not for me. For some reason, even though God was not for me, I had a Bible commentary I had found on a sidewalk that I read each night. After reading, I would write down every word on my hole-punched paper and then put it into an old notebook. I felt safe reading this Bible commentary instead of the Bible.

The Lover of my soul knew it would be just a matter of time when my days of running from Him would be over. The church I visited that Sunday began to shorten that time. So on that very first visit, as I sat in the pews in one of those stolen skirt and vest sets, I heard the pastor announce they needed a teacher for the kindergarten class. For some reason, I raised my hand. I am still not sure why I did that. I think the real me that loves adventure and starting new things sprouted up. The preacher, I assumed, did not know I was not a member of the church, because, after the service, he gave me the Sunday school material and sent me on my way.

Years later, as I grew in my Christian walk, the Lover of my soul brought the theft of those two skirt sets back to my memory and called for restitution. When I told Him the mall had closed down, He noted the department store was closed in Chattanooga but not in other cities. So I found a location of the Miller Brothers Department Store in Knoxville, Tennessee.

I had no clue of how much the stolen items cost, but I wrote the check for a certain amount with a letter explaining I had stolen from their store, I was now a Christian, and I needed to pay for the items I had taken. Signed, sealed and, I guess, delivered. The letter with the check in it was never returned to me. I honestly can't remember if someone from Miller Brothers' ever cashed the check.

As I went home with the Sunday school materials, I realized it was the first time in a long time I actually had my hands on a Bible. It took me back to Momma reading it to us when I was young. I became so excited to teach the next Sunday.

That Sunday morning, I arrived at the church early. I was shown the room where I was to teach. I placed the lesson book on the desk and set the crayons, paper, and scissors on the table designated for our activity time. I could hardly wait till the little students arrive.

Their mothers began to drop them off one by one. Some screamed to go back with their mothers while others ran to the activity table. It took a few minutes for me to get everyone calm. I told them about the wonderful time we would have. They promised they would be quiet as I told them the lesson, and I promised them some yummy snacks after the lesson. I could not wait to teach them how to memorize the Bible verse for that week. I was full of pride as we started with a song.

But the joke was on me: those Kindergarteners knew more about scriptures than I did. There was no way I would let a bunch of Kindergarteners be smarter than I. So I began studying the Bible.

Almost every day, something was going on at church, and I was there. I was a single, working parent with two young children and no car. Church services did not go by a clock, and sometimes we were there a long time.

With no car of my own, I had to wait for someone to take me home.

My children often wondered why we could not go home as their playmates had done with their parents. They were too young to understand I was trying to keep every law and be obedient to earn God's love. So it did not matter to me how long we stayed because I did not want the Lord to leave me or disappear forever.

Even after several years on my Christian journey, the loss of security I had suffered as a child continued to cloud my mind. Any sense of real security was long gone. My life became so unstable after Momma died.

One part of me lived in fear that something else awful would happen while the other part would sprout up and start on the road of hope again. Those childhood fears still confused and puzzled me. I thought God would be angry if I missed a church service and did something with the kids instead. Guilt kicked my butt and fear was its overseer. I thought God would never forgive me for saying He did not exist.

However, I found the biggest fear was the fear of people themselves. My childhood life had been filled with so many adults telling me what I could or could not do. If there were a club called "Others Could—We Cannot," I would have been the president for sure. I remembered my friend Angela told me about a job opening where she worked. I had an interview thanks to her influence, and I got there a couple of hours early. We ate breakfast in the large cafeteria. After giving me directions and instructions, she headed for her department, and I took the elevator to the lobby to wait for my set appointment. I looked down from the elevator and saw numerous people entering the building. Some were walking fast, others laughed and talked as they hurried to their departments. By the time the elevator stopped, the lobby was full of people dressed in business attire. The fear of people overcame me. I panicked and left. I did not attend the interview.

WHERE CAN I FIND LOVE?

For God so loved the World that He gave His only Son, that whoever believes in Him shall not perish, but have eternal life.

-John 3:16

English Standard Version

It had been almost five years since I first raised my hand to teach the kindergarten class. Now I was teaching the adult Sunday school class. I found myself afraid of the adults that were in positions of authority, such as the elders and the pastor. I began to act just like I did as a child. I constantly reminded myself to just do what this or that adult told me to do. I unconsciously allowed others to control my life.

My friend Vanessa was the first person to invite me to Precept Ministries. Founded by Jack and Kay Arthur, Precept Ministries is a non-denominational place where Christians could come to study and grow closer to God. We would go to one of the small group classes first, and then everyone would meet in the auditorium to hear Kay speak. Just like being taught how to dissect a frog in biology, we were taught how to dissect a book of the Bible—one chapter and one verse at a time. I was fascinated by such learning. We studied Judges, Philippians, and 2nd Timothy. However, it was the class "Marriage Without

Regrets" that awakened my need to know more about God and His love. Vanessa and her fiancé had registered for the course. Halfway through the class, her fiancé got a job assignment out of town. So I took his place.

My first time in the class, the chapter we discussed was about the four types of love—agape, philia, eros, and storge. The one that interested me the most was the agape love. According to *Strong's Concordance*, agape (God's love) is love given whether it is returned or not; the person continues to love, even without any self-benefits, to will the good of another.

I read the homework scripture in Romans 5:8: "But God showed his love for us in that while we were still sinners, Christ died for us." I was still not sure if I would ever really feel that kind of love. I felt like Mary, the mother of Jesus, who pondered about Jesus in her heart. I pondered about what I heard and read about Jesus and His love. I began to think it was possible for God to love me.

There was a lot for me to learn about this love. I became hungry and thirsty for it. As I read the Bible, I concentrated and meditated on the pages. I began to see glimpses of who I was not and the person God planned for me to be. I began to understand if God really loved the world, then I was included in that love.

After Vanessa married, I continued to go to other classes at Precept with other friends. Strange as it seems, the more I studied the Bible, the more it conflicted with how I felt. I knew God loved me because he loves everyone. To me, that was too general. He does love everybody. However, there was still a longing to know He really loved me for me. I could not let go of the fear I might do something to lose His love.

My mindset had not changed from the belief that others had privileges I did not have. They had parents. They were not restricted by the color of their skin. They did not have things taken away from them just because of who they were. I thought agape love may have been one of those privileges I would never have. So I continued to focus on the law of God's word without the heart of His word. Once again, just like as a child, I was obeying those in authority, no questions asked. At this time, it was what I believed was the authority of God.

My studies at Precept paid off. I became the Sunday School Superintendent at church. Yet I had an overwhelming list of questions floating in my head. It was this overly worked questionnaire in my head concerning God's unconditional love triggered a strong desire to talk to someone. One day after Precept class, I discussed my inner turmoil at work with Wanda. She suggested I make an appointment with Molly, a counselor who taught our Monday evening class. In class, there was no question too silly to ask concerning our lesson. Before I even knew she was a counselor, I thought of her as someone I could talk to about personal things. I wanted to silence some fears that continuously came to mind, so I made the call.

The counseling session was on a Tuesday. Wanda picked me up to make sure I did not change my mind. She gave me a big hug and spoke a quick prayer before I entered Molly's office, but I was still nervous.

I opened the door to Molly's office with a shaky hand. I was frightened. I closed the door, took a deep breath, and thanked her for seeing me. Her appearance made me think there should be a halo over her head. She stood up, shook my hand, and asked me to sit in the chair that faced the one she rose from. She told me about herself, and we discussed how I liked the classes. Next, she gave me an overview of what to expect and prayed concerning our time together.

"Velma," she said, "Tell me about you. Start from childhood to now."

So, I began my counseling session. When I finished, I felt relieved. Even her flowery wallpaper no longer seemed too busy. She took my hands, leaned closer to me, and in the sweetest, consoling voice she said, "You are suffering from a severe case of rejection. You are having a hard time believing anyone loves you. Because you do not believe anyone loves you, you can't believe God loves you either."

Then she began to tell me about the love of God. When she finished, she asked me if I wanted that love. If I said yes, I would be accepting God Himself because God is love. With tears flowing down my cheeks, I whispered, "Yes." Again, she prayed. Then I prayed. Afterward, I opened my eyes with a broad smile on my face. My search for love was over. Molly told me, I did not ever have to worry about someone loving me again. I had the Spirit of the Creator of the universe living inside me. He would fill my heart with so much compassion that I could love others the way He loves me.

I sat there silently for a moment or two in complete amazement. God really loves me, I thought. Wow, He loves me. I could not stop thinking about it. I needed to go home and talk to Him more. I stood up, gave her a big hug and thanked her for her time and compassion. This time, I opened the door with a steady and strong hand. I walked out of her office with a different spring in my step than when I went in.

I had waited a few minutes before I called Wanda to pick me up. Before she arrived, I thought about the drive to my house. I really had no time to talk. Anticipation of being alone with The Lover of my Soul was all I wanted to do.

MY NEW BIRTH, MY OLD WAYS

For I do not understand my own actions. For I do not do what I want, but I do the very thing I hate.

-Romans 7:15

English Standard Version

After I promised Wanda I would tell her all about the counseling session the next day, we said our goodbyes, and I hurried into the house. At the time, my oldest brother was staying with me for a couple of weeks. He had cleaned the kitchen, and the children were in bed. After going to their room to see if they were asleep, I went to my room and closed the door. I started to sit in my chair near my bed. I wanted to humble myself, so I sat on the floor at the foot of my bed. I sat there in amazement as Molly's words began to echo through my head. "God is love. His love is unconditional."

"He loves me. He really loves me." I whispered those words over and over. "He loves me. He really loves me." My blouse was wet with tears of joy that flowed from my eyes.

Finally I asked Him, "You loved me when I rejected you? You loved me even when I fornicated? When I lied, or when I told people you were not real?"

At that moment, as if time stood still, I heard a resounding "Yes, Yes, Yes!"

"Okay, so you are telling me if I were to have sex with my boyfriend right now, you would still love me?" I asked Him.

I had to see this for myself. My Gideon test began. I called my boyfriend, and drove my brother's car to his house, and lay in his bed ready to fulfill his sexual needs. My heart held on to the small doubt that the Lover of my soul would actually stay around after I committed this sin.

Afterward, I waited for His wrath, the scolding, and the rightful rejection. It did not happen. I thought maybe after I went home, I would experience that rejection. It did not occur that night or the next. He did not turn his back on me. In fact, the Lover of my soul actually blessed me. He did not stop loving me. I felt His presence. I was used to men walking away even when I did all the right things, and unquestionably not staying around when I did not. This man Jesus was truly like no one I had ever encountered.

After I had realized I could not deny that love anymore, I found myself the next week once again at the foot of my bed. But this time, I was sorrowful for acting so foolishly. I closed my eyes and ruminated on the change in my life. I sat on the cold, shiny, vinyl, bedroom floor puzzled. It was my time to talk to God. I prayed. This unhurried time in prayer again revealed His love and my need for His love. My soul had a new Lover now. He had given me a new life, a new nature—His. Once again, I found myself overjoyed, enthused, and relieved.

Before this night, I thought I had no life. Now I had a new life and somehow an old life. Confusing, huh? Tell me about it. This new life and the old life were entangled in the midst of no life. What a dilemma! I wish I could say from the time of that prayer, I understood God and everything was great from then on, but the truth of the matter is, I did not.

Unknown to me at the time, this was the beginning of an inner war within me and the only one who could help me conquer it was the God who promised to never leave nor forsake me. For those who struggle with rejection, your fall back mindset is: *"they will leave."* God had His work cut out for me. The Spirit of Rejection was at war with my faith in God's love for me.   Thank God the battle was not mine.

THE WAR DEEP WITHIN

We use God's mighty weapons, not worldly weapons, to knock down the strongholds of human reasoning and to destroy false arguments.

II Corinthians 10:4

New Living Translation NLT

Knowing He loves me and living through His love was an ongoing process. Now that I was a Christian, I had a new life. Unspeakable joy and peace filled my heart. I accepted the truth that Jesus had died, was buried, and rose from the dead. His Spirit was alive in me. I was born again. I was a new babe in Christ. For the first time in my life, hope flourished in every fiber of my being. I knew I had a lifetime plus eternity to know God. All I wanted to do was please Him out of my love for Him because He first loved me. I no longer feared God would leave me if I did not please Him by coming to church every day or not doing everything those in authority asked. Putting a smile on the Lover of my soul's face brought me great joy.

The Velma that had been shaped and formed into a hopeless, rejected, angry, bitter, and resentful person was no longer in control.

I began to see the internal war between my old mindset and the newly developing one. I was naïve to think all my old thoughts would instantly go away. The enemy of my soul was not going to raise the white flag of surrender. He had held me captive since my childhood. He started an invisible war deep within me. The natural eye could not see it. In fact, not one of my five senses could discern what was going on. They were pawns under the enemy's control.

Nevertheless, the Lover of my soul had defeated and annulled any grip this crafty enemy had on me. Now that I was a new person in Him, victory was mine. Jesus gave His life so I would be set free from behind the enemy's line. The Lover of my soul knew the plans He had for me. He intended for my good and not evil, to give me a hope and future. Because I belonged to Jesus, He promised to send a Comforter—His Holy Spirit—to teach me and guide me. I no longer had to rely on my five senses. I could rely on His Spirit. The Spirit of my Lover would use my natural senses the way the Creator had designed. I was instructed, as all Christians are, to draw closer to Him. This intimate relationship would increase my awareness of His presence concerning Jesus, His Father, and His Spirit. My alone time with Him, learning His voice, heeding His instruction, and confronted by His presence, began to transform me from the grip of fear and rejection. To know Him and somehow make Him known became the longing cry of my heart. I developed an unquenchable thirst to know more of His ways, His truths. I continued to read His written words in the Bible. Afterward I would sing, sometimes dance, and let Him know how much I loved Him.

There were times when I had to confess I listened to the enemy instead of Him. His response was always reassuring. I would sit still and listen to His familiar voice instructing me concerning what He was doing for me and through me, turning me around once again to follow His Spirit. Because my old ways were embedded deep within my soul, it was so refreshing to trust this omnipotent God to set me free indeed.

Until this point, the enemy of my soul had used three things to establish the foundation of a false identity within me. They were my family origin, my race, and my social status. This enemy wanted more than a foothold in my heart. From my beginning, he wanted to be its master.

From the moment I glided through the birth canal into the delivery room, my family dynamic defined and shaped my identity. The security of Momma's hugs and kisses, her provision and love for us, provided a safe place for me. I was loved and accepted. On the other hand, her death suddenly removed that security I had known. After her death, Satan's whispers replaced security with doubt, fear and inferiority. Before long, I was an unlovable victim, incapable of trusting anyone or anything.

The second brick Satan used in the foundation of false identity that shaped my belief system was my race. Outside the safety of my family, I was identified by the dark color of my skin. Light skinned blacks were considered prettier, more popular, and widely accepted. I heard things like "You are so black," "You are pretty for a dark skinned girl."

Unconsciously, the lie that someone was better than me because they were lighter took residence within me. The times spent with Momma Lesli and living on "our" side of town had a significant impact on how I viewed the world and my place in it. I had a distorted and false sense of who I could be. Seeds of inferiority were planted, and I bore its fruit with every limitation I placed on myself.

Social status, the third brick of this false belief, was also used by the father of lies. Where we had to live, what school we could attend, and who we could play with all impacted me. The forced poverty we suffered spoke volumes about my significance in this world. The enemy of my soul used these lies to imprison my heart. I was stuck in my own reactions concerning my childhood wounds.

Dr. David Banks, a pastor, and a life coach helped me understand why I was so stuck. As we sat in Panera Bread one morning, I told him about a dream I had concerning my Momma's funeral. He listened intensely while sipping his coffee. I described how amazed I was of all the things I had forgotten and what I had discovered since the dream. He placed the cup to his lips, sipped his last drop and pressed his lips together as he enjoyed the taste. He then set the cup back on the table and began to speak in a very calm, pastoral voice and said -

"Velma, trauma is a deep-seated grief. Grief was developed to go through a process. If you and I do not know the process, we get stuck."

"Arrested Development," is what he called it. It hinders emotional development. He used his coaching skills to illustrate how emotional retardation can remain even into adulthood. He then asked me if I understood.

"Wow," I replied.

My eyes of understanding began to open. I was stuck for sure. I explained to him how often I wondered what was wrong with me. At times, the expression of love from another person was difficult for me to receive. For example, my response to a simple compliment was often mechanical. It was as if I needed permission to express all of my emotions. Dr. Banks continued with more illustrations on trauma. He pointed out that those of us who have gone through childhood trauma match our identity based on our experience. He further explained if we let the experiences go, then the identity we had come to believe was our true self would be gone. If we let them go, then what would become of our identity?

What was a Christian to do? It was like going to war with the necessary weapons, but with no knowledge of what the enemy looked like. The Holy Spirit made it possible for me to not only see the enemy's devices, but also how to call on God when I was truly ready to make a change from the old reactions to a new way of responding.

I remember a visit to Ms. Moore's house, (Vanessa's mom) one Easter Sunday. I do not remember how I was dressed or the sermon that was preached at church. What I do remember is my reaction concerning a compliment I received from Ms. Moore. She was a classy lady. Her attire was stately, her nails polished, and her hair always looked as if she had a personal stylist at home. She was fun to be with, and I stopped at her house for a short visit.

As she walked me to my car, she complimented me on how beautiful I looked in in my dress. Unbeknownst to me, I frowned. She turned me around and gave a matter of fact stare. In a lady-like yet stern voice, she spoke words that pierced my heart.

"I will never give you a compliment again," she said. "Every time I say something kind to you, you frown. Sweetie, I am through."

I got in my car with tears in my eyes. I went home, looked into the mirror and asked my soul's Lover how could people expect me to smile. Before He showed me how, He enlightened me on why I was afraid to smile. The memories of when I was in the ninth grade surfaced. I just received my ninth-grade school pictures. I was so proud, but it was short lived. The first person I showed them to was a young man who told me not to ever smile again. It made me look ugly. The enemy used the words of that young man to imprison me in my heart. From that time, I had reacted by working hard not to smile again. However, that evening, with help from the God, not only did I smile, but I laughed until my jaws hurt. That was one mindset that would no longer hold me captive. Smiling became a work in progress. From that day forward, trusting Him was my heart's desire. Slowly but surely, I was changing into the person I was purposed to be—and smiling at that.

THE LIGHT AT THE END OF THE TUNNEL

And we know that for those who love God all things work together for good, for those who are called according to His purpose.

-Romans 8:28

English Standard Version

The key to obeying God is to forgive. I am overjoyed that I can say I have forgiven the man who caused such pain in my life when I was 15 years old. It took three verbal confrontations with him to finally realize thorns surround roses.

The first encounter came about from a conversation on the riverbank with my hair stylist. He loved to go fishing and would always go when he had a day off. He called me one day and asked if I wanted to learn how to fish. I hesitated at first, the thought of touching worms made me frown. At the end of our talk, I had promised him I would come. When I arrived, he had already caught one of two fish he called – brims. He had my fishing rod baited. He was excited as he instructed me on how to cast the rod further in the water. I sat in an awkward position on a big rock after I cast. He gave me advice on how to reel the rod in once I got a bite and assured me he would help me. As he talked, I looked at the water and the surrounding trees;

everything was so beautiful and peaceful except for the constant drone of my hair stylist's voice like a fly buzzing in my ear.

He asked me to get something out of his tackle box and although I hated the thought of having any contact with worms I grudgingly tread my way towards the box. Suddenly and without any warning, he asked me who was the father of my daughter. I kept walking like I did not hear him. However, he asked me again. Walking back with the plastic container in my hand and my heart thumping fast, I told him the fourteen-year-old lie concerning who the father was. He replied, *"You know that is not true." "You think nobody knows what happen to you, but the young man did come to school the next day and told a lot of guys what happened."* He went on to tell me it would be best to tell my daughter the truth. He explained she did not need to find out from a stranger or in the midst of a medical emergency, such as needing blood because of an accident or health problem.

I handed him the plastic container and sat back down on my awkward rock. Speaking about awkward, I was confronted with an awkward situation. The secret was never a secret after all. What was I to do? I held the fishing pole tighter than I was instructed to do. A fish was no longer what I had to catch. I needed a hope and prayer this truth would be handled the right way for my daughter's sake.

At home, I thought about what just happened. After getting over the shock, I prayed for wisdom. I knew God, in His sovereignty, was in control of the matter and it was time to live in truth.

What came to mind was the day I was so angry at God. I reflected back when I shouted to God that He was the giver of life, and He would have to make this baby special. Well, He did just that.

I prayed God would give me the courage and boldness to do what must be done. I did not know how it was going to unfold, but through fasting and prayer, I knew I would do what must be done. I could no longer just say I forgive. I had to put it into action.

A week later, my hair stylist called and gave me a telephone number to call. He said I would know who it was when I made the call. After our goodbyes, I wondered why he would give me a number to call and not tell me who it was. I placed the number on my dresser. Weeks afterward, I was looking for something and saw the paper. Curiosity got the best of me, so I picked up the receiver and dialed the telephone number.

The voice on the other end of the phone was a surprise indeed. The lady who said hello was the girlfriend of the young man I needed to forgive. My heart sunk, yet my courage kicked in. I indeed knew what to do. She and I talked about how we had not seen each other since high school. Then I asked her if the young man was there. Her reply was, "no." She did ask me if he had my telephone number. I boldly gave her my phone and requested she would ask him to call me because I had something to discuss concerning when we were in school.

He did not call me back that day, but eventually he did. It was the right time because I had just completed my fast. I felt like I was in charge, and I would do what I needed to be set free once and for all. My daughter's future depended on me not being scared.

Believe it or not, I was so bold that I picked him up from his girlfriend's house and drove to a public park. Along the way, he talked about how he had not seen me in years. I did not say a word. I think he told me he had moved out of town in our twelfth-grade school year. I thought blocking him out of my mind was the reason I had not seen him.

I was the driver. That gave me internal security. I drove to DuPont Park in Hixson. I felt safe in a public place. I parked in the center of the park surrounded by people. I didn't have to pick my daughter until up after a school game, so

I had plenty of time. I had the bible in my hands when I began to talk.

I explained how I got his girlfriend's telephone number and how I needed to discuss something with him. I was nervous. I silently prayed I would stay courageous. I thought what was I thinking to pick him up and bring him to this park. It was too late now; we were there.

Stumbling over my words, I reminded him of that day I was at his house. You best believe I gave every detail of what took place. I did not let the knot in my stomach stop me. I held on to the Bible more tightly as I got to the part of the result of his horrible foolish actions. I told him I had a child. There it was out. The knot in my stomach was not so tight anymore. He looked up at me and said "He did not have any child support money." That's when I got mad. I informed him I did not need his money. She was well taken care of. I had to calm myself down. So I blurted out how I had hated him all these years. It was hard not to be angry. Again, I had to calm down. Finally, I shared that I was a Christian now and had to forgive. My anger began to soften, and I thought about his salvation.

Had there been a change in him as there was in me? That thought vanished when his reply was, "You should be glad I did not have a "train," ran on you like other girls had." Back in the day, it meant multiple boys were taking what the girl did not give them permission to take.

Although those words cut into emotions I didn't not know I had, I ignored what he said. "I have to forgive you," I said. "I have to tell my daughter and I did not want this hatred in my heart any longer."

I wanted to believe he felt the sincerity in my heart and a desperate need to forgive. I quoted some scriptures and looked at my watch. I did not have long to take him back home and pick my daughter up from school. We sat in silence for a minute or two. He spoke. This time he said he was sorry, and he was a "messed up" person back then. He hoped one day he would find this Jesus I talked about. He told me about his mother's church.

The more he talked. The more at peace I became. I did what I had planned to do. I said face-to-face – "I forgive you." I had taken control of my life. It would take two more confrontations before the emotions would finally settle to true forgiveness.

I get to smell the roses now without being hurt by the thorns. He apologized for his past behavior, and I have forgiven him. My prayer is that God has become his Lover also.

I visited the cemetery where Momma was buried. I did not find her actual gravesite. However, I was able to make peace that day. My next step is to have the memorial service that took place in my dreams.

SOWING AND REAPING

Do not be deceived: God is not mocked, for whatever one sows, that will he also reap.

-Galatians 6:7
English Standard Version

A Tribute to Those Who Helped Along the Way

What the enemy meant for evil, Christ worked out for good. Dornita, (Hatchet), my sister-parent, paused her life and took on the enormous responsibility of raising her brothers and sisters. She did not drown herself in self-pity as I did. She continued with her dreams in spite of her circumstances. I am forever grateful for her love and influence in my life.

She married her daughter's father after our youngest brother graduated and enlisted in the army. They have another daughter and three grandchildren. November 4, 2008, she was awarded "Teacher of the Year" in Norfolk, VA. In receiving such an honor, she was invited to the White House and met President Barack Obama and First Lady Michelle Obama.

The young man who helped me raise my daughter demonstrated such unconditional love beyond my expectations by claiming a child he knew was not his. Although I was blind to that kind of love, I will forever treasure the friendship we now have. It is true, you reap what you sow. My prayer for him is he reaps seven-fold the love he showed me.

THE HEART OF THE ISSUE

Don't copy the behavior and customs of this world, but let God transform you into a new person by changing the way you think. Then you will learn to know God's will for you, which is good and pleasing and perfect.

—Romans 12:2

New Living Translation (NLT)

THE DREAM

On January 6, 2014, I had a dream that put all my "I "Can nots" into perspective on why it seems like I do not belong in this group, or in this program or church. Why can't I express my joys or my likes? Why am I always thinking of the next thing before I get through with what I am doing? Why do I hesitate to make a decision?

This is the dream I shared with Dr. Banks:

The dream I told him began with a neighbor knocking on our front door. The house was the house we grew up in at Maurice Poss Homes. He said that someone was giving my mom a memorial. "Why after all these years," I asked. He said he did not know why. They just said we needed to be there. He told me to make sure I tell my oldest sister and my youngest brother. So I did as well as the others. It was like we were all living in the same house.

I dressed, and while waiting for the others, I saw my friend, Pam, as I waited outside. Pam asked me to walk with her and the young lady she was helping. They were walking to the massage therapy facility where Pam had made her appointment. When we got to the place, it looked like Warehouse Row, *an upscale retail shop on Market Street. Pam told me she had to go, so I would have to take the young lady upstairs. So I did.*

When I got upstairs, although Pam had paid for the young lady, the employees were not sure they wanted to wait on this young lady. She was very tall. She wore a very short dress and boots. She looked like a lady of the night. She instantly became angry and let the receptionist know it. I walked her out of the room and told her she had a problem dealing with anger and she needed to see a counselor. She said she did see one and it was not helping. I told her about a counselor that would help her.

We went to another floor for her to be waited on. When we got there, again we were told she should not be there yet. I told them I had to go, so the receptionist said she would take care of the young lady. The young lady said she really wanted to go to the memorial with me. I told her she could not come dressed the way she was, but somehow her dress became long with grass stains at the bottom. I told her we could work it out, but I needed to go because I did not want to be late for the memorial.

Now I do not know if what happened next was before or after I met the lady, but I entered into a room, and there was a crowd of people listening to preachers. I sat there and listened as well. I learned there were different preachers... The facilitator asked if anyone else had something to say. I began to speak for about 5 or 10 minutes and then I sat down. Everyone clapped.

I looked at my watch and knew I had to leave. So I got up and said, "Excuse me," to a lady sitting next to me. She said to me, "I did not understand a word you said." Another got up next to her and said the same thing. I told them both the reason was that I was not a preacher, but a teacher. A teacher breaks down the scriptures so you will understand the context of it.

143

The lady still did not understand—so I gave her an example of how a word in one verse does not mean the same in another verse. After explaining what I taught earlier, she then understood and thanked me. She also asked me to come back.

I left and decided to go out the back way because it took longer for us to exit using the front entrance. Once outside, I entered a big field. There was a man I knew in my younger years standing as a guard by the fence. He told me something, and then he walked to the back. I turned to see where he had gone, and I thought surely the "preacher" was not doing something illegal. I looked at my watch and thought, "I must get home. I must get to the memorial."

Somehow I was now in a car. I got in, and then I woke up. I laid there to see if I could go back to sleep and finish the dream. I fell back asleep, and the dream continued.

I was still trying to get to my family so I could get us to the memorial. Then, the dream took me to my mom's funeral. My principal told someone to take us younger kids home, because if we could not handle the funeral, how could we handle the gravesite? So someone took us to our house. There were many people there and lots of food. I do not know if the dinner was being served at the church or our house.

The next thing I remember is looking at a picture of me. I had on my favorite dress—lavender, with the upper part being white and lavender. My hair was neatly combed, and I looked so pretty. I posed for the picture with my hands down. I really liked that dress and the way I looked.

Then I remembered the last thing my Momma said to me. She told me one day I would have a bedroom of my own. She told me to go to the five-and-dime store to buy some plastic curtains with my uncle. She gave me the money and told me not to give it to him. She did not trust him.

Then I woke up again. It was 6:30, so I thought I would get up at 7:00. I went back to sleep. In my dream, I had finally made it back home. I thought I had missed the memorial. I thought about how I never got to tell my youngest brother about Momma's gravesite as I opened the door to enter the house. To my surprise, my neighbor and his wife were eating a fish plate meal at our table or was it their table? Robert told me I had missed the memorial. I was so sad and fearful because I knew my oldest sister would be upset. I asked if they had any programs. After saying yes, he got up, found one, and gave it to me.

I looked at the memorial program, and the first thing I saw was she died at age 47. That was wrong. I went to my room and tried not to awaken anyone. I looked again at the program and noticed the picture on the front. It was so colorful. It was a picture of our kitchen table with food on it; spotless and pretty.

The program suddenly turned into a video. Everything was so incredibly clean and pretty. I went down the hall into the kitchen which was big. There were two kitchen tables. The sink was filled with food Momma was preparing for dinner. It looked like there was plenty of food. Wow, I thought. Everything was plentiful and beautiful.

I took off my coat. I was filled with sadness and gladness. I tried to play some music but had the wrong cord for the stereo. By now, my daughter was walking down the hall and, behind her, my niece. My daughter began to fuss at me for missing the memorial and said "Mom, you're always missing something." But my niece interrupted her and said, "Your mom always focuses on the inward of the heart, trying to help somebody or something like that."

Whatever else she said, it calmed my daughter down. She handed me another program and said, "You all did not win first place." I asked her what she meant by that since this was a memorial and not a contest. I opened the program again, and it looked like Christmas trees and decorations. They were beautiful. I asked what it meant, but she did not answer.

By this time, my oldest sister awakened. I knew she would be mad. I was so sorry. I had let other things get in the way. My oldest sister told me Hatchet did not come.

Then the dream went to a book— I'd read. In one particular chapter, the author found closure at his Dad's gravesite. I felt like I needed to find closure also, and that is when I remembered that I never went to Momma's gravesite. Years back, I had called the cemetery office and asked where my mother was buried. I was told they did not have a record of that because it had been such a long time ago. I knew then I would have to find out before I woke up.

I had one more memory: not going to the gravesite the day of the funeral and my elementary principal, saying we did not need to go. The other one was the picture of me in that beautiful purple and white dress. The picture reminded me of the time when I thought I was not pretty... I either had it on at the funeral or Easter. In the dream, I was told to go back to the chapter where the author found closure. I woke up this time for good.

I sat in bed in disbelief. What in the world did I just dream? Was I asleep or did I get a visit from the Spirit of God? I grabbed a pen and paper and immediately wrote down all the above.

My head became filled with floods of memories. I finally put the pen and paper away. I still could not move out of the bed. So I asked God questions only He could answer. An hour later, I got dressed and called my sister, Judy. I knew she would tell me some of the things I needed to know. She did just that. Two days later I went to the downtown library and got a copy of Momma's obituary.

The Bible says in Luke 6:45, "The good person out of the good treasure of his heart produces good, and the evil person out of his evil treasures produce evil, for out of the abundance of the heart, the mouth speaks."

When I had the dream concerning Momma's death, I knew it was a tool used to unlock the fear within. Unrecognized trauma had left a big void in my heart and mind. What I did not know or remember was hurting me because the voids were being filled with twisted truths—in other words, lies. They had been a part of me for so long, and I would never have thought they were actually false beliefs. These false beliefs had blocked the truth from taking root in my heart.

The mind is like the monitor of a computer. A monitor can only show what is in the hardware. Without my soul's Lover, my mind operated from a damaged, or should I say, a "dead," soul. The memories that were stored in my mind reflected the thoughts that had formulated from my heart. The storage process began at birth. Stored memories of different, circumstances, events and situations and my initial reactions to them set the pattern of who I once was. This way of thinking shaped my natural belief system and created my own identity crisis. My soul's enemy used them so well in my life that I concluded I was worthless. I did not know my

Lover's purpose: From the very beginning, I was born to be born again.

My problem was uncovered: I had no self-identity. I only existed. There was no one to blame except myself. I believed the lies from the enemy. He used the pain and hurt to build within me an inner wall of self-pity. I praise God for the revelation that my experiences no longer defined me. I have an identity. It is not based on my race or social classification. It is not even based on what I have done wrong or right. I am who I am because of Jesus Christ.

What I did not get from my earthly father, my Heavenly Father gave through His Son. He has freely given me love, acceptance, and significance. I know who I am. Without a pinch of doubt, I know God created me in His image and likeness. That was God's most precious blessing—Himself. I belong to the family of God. I have His Identity.

While the enemy used trauma as a way to keep me in bondage, God took those painfully stored memories and wounds and freed my mind from their effects. My identity is now grounded in Christ. The Spirit of Christ now lives within me. He is mine, and I am His. It is pleasing to have Him within me. Our intimate relationship grows every day. I talk to Him about everything. The whispers I now hear are from the One who created me. He tells me how fearfully and wonderfully I am made. He shares with me how He delights in my heart's desires. The greatest part of prayer for me is allowing God time to talk to me. It has been through these profound personal moments with my Savior I have been given the faith to trust Him fully.

I AM WHO I AM

I have been crucified with Christ; and it is no longer I who live, but Christ lives in me; and the life which I now live in the flesh I live by faith in the Son Of God, who loved me and gave Himself up for me.

-Galatians 2:20

New American Standard Bible

I now view myself differently. I no longer allow my experiences to define me. The Lord is my Creator. Therefore, I am His. I am a beautiful woman. I am naturally smart and intelligent. I have divine wisdom that leads me and guides me.

I have many roles in my life. I am a mother, a wife, and a grandmother. I am a sister, an auntie, and a friend. I am an entrepreneur and a writer. I fulfill all these roles in my life through my relationship with my Lord.

- I am a Daughter of the Most High God
- I am a woman of purpose
- I am a servant leader
- I am an Agent of Change
- I am an author
- I am a Woman of Excellence
- I am an inspiration to those who are captive to their past

- I am trustworthy
- I am humble
- I am kind
- I am focused
- I value people
- I am loved
- I am supportive
- I am assertive

THE WORD BECAME FLESH

He sent out His word and healed them, and delivered them from their destructions.

-Psalms 107:20

English Standard Version

Trauma can arrest your emotions and hold them captive. It does not matter whether it is a parents' death, physical abuse, emotional abuse, or bullying. Read the following statements. Check any that may describe your thoughts or feelings.

❑　I feel like I do not fit in when I am in a group

❑ I feel lonely

❑ I feel like I must do what others want me to do so I can be accepted

❑ I feel bad about myself

❑ I feel stressed when I am the center of attention

❑ I stay hiding in the background to escape being noticed

❑ I feel if I drink alcohol or use drugs I will feel better about myself

❑ I feel I should be over my parents' passing by now

❑ I feel what happened to me is my fault

❑ I am an angry all the time, but I do not know why

❑ I feel like I have to stay busy at all the times

If you checked any of these, the Lover of your soul wants to heal you from your past hurts. You can talk to your pastor or a counselor.

I have included the scriptures on the following pages to comfort your heart. This is your time to embrace the freedom to be yourself, who you were created to be.

"Yet it was our grief He bore, or sorrows that weighed him down. And we thought His troubles were a punishment from God for his own sins? But He was wounded and bruised for our sins. He was beaten that we might have peace; He was lashed—and we were healed! We—every one of us—have strayed away like a ship! We, who left God's paths to follow our own. Yet God laid on Him the guilt and sins of every one of us!"
Isaiah 53:4-6
Living Bible (TLB)

"I will comfort you there as a little one is comforted by its mother."
Isaiah 66:13
Living Bible (TLB)

"And the Lord will guide you continually, and satisfy you with all good things, and keep you healthy too; and you will like a well-garden, like an ever-flowing spring."
Isaiah 58:11
Living Bible (TLB)

Velma Wilson

"You have sorrow now, but I will see you again and then you will rejoice, and one can rob you of that joy."
John 16:22
Living Bible (TLB)

MEET THE LOVER OF YOUR SOUL

For God so loved the world, that He gave His only Son, that whoever believe in Him should not perish but have eternal life.

-John 3:16

New English Standard

JESUS THE CHRIST

"For God So Loved the World that, He gave His only Son that whoever believes in him should not perish but shall have eternal life."
John 3:16
English Standard Version

"She will give birth to a son, and you are to give him the name Jesus because he will save his people from their sins."
Matthew 1:21
New International Version

"Neither is there salvation in any other: for there is none other name under heaven given among men, whereby we must be saved."
Acts 4:12
King James Bible

"So we have come to know and have believed the love that God has for us. God is love, and the one who abides in God and God abides in him." I John 4:16
English Standard Version

YOUR RESPONSE

For all have sinned and fall short of the glory of God.

Roman 3:23

English Standard Version

"If you confess with your mouth that Jesus is Lord and believe in your heart that God raised him from the dead, you will be saved."
New Living translation (TLB) Romans 10:9

Below is the prayer I prayed when I received the Lover of my soul into my heart.

My Prayer

Jesus. I thank you for loving me. I confess with my mouth and believe in my heart that God raised you from the dead. I repent of my sins and ask you to come into my heart. Thank you that I am now in the family of God.

You can pray this prayer or one similar to this one. You can also contact a pastor to assist you.

Please feel free to contact me.

I would love to hear from you. My email address is: msvelmawilson@gmail.com

Use the following pages to reflect upon your own life.

What has caused you to be anything other than what you were created to be?

_____

_____

_____

_____

_____

_____

_____

_____

_____

_____

_____

_____

_____

_____

_____

_____

_____

_____

_____

_____

How will you make an effort to find your path and allow the Lover of your soul to show you the plans He has for you?

_____

_____

_____

_____

_____

_____

_____

_____

_____

_____

_____

_____

_____

_____

_____

_____

_____

_____

Use the space below to write your own "I Am" statements!

_____

_____

_____

_____

_____

_____

_____

_____

_____

_____

_____

_____

_____

_____

_____

_____

_____

_____

_____

_____

_____

_____

_____

References

Books

Chambers, Oswald, Biblical Psychology 1995
Oswald Chambers Publication's Association

Scazzero, Geri, The Emotionally Heathy
Woman
2010 Zondervan

Elliott, Elizabeth, Loneliness 1988 Thomas
Nelson Publishers Nashville

Bible Quotes
Bible quotes and scriptures taken from Bible
Hub Online Parallel Bible – Bible-Hub.com

Holman Christian Standard Bible
English Stand Version
King James Version

GOD'S WORD Translation

ABOUT THE AUTHOR

Velma Wilson is a native of Chattanooga, Tennessee, where she continues to reside. She is an award-winning entrepreneur and realtor. She has received community honors, recognitions, and awards for her business and service to the community.

She received her Bachelor of Science degree from Covenant College. Velma received a certification in Theology from Interdenominational Theological Center – (ITC) Chattanooga Campus and is a certified Christian Counselor.

Velma is a servant leader who has counseled career women, teen mothers, and women who are incarcerated.

Velma is the proud wife of Bobby. They have two children - a daughter who is an attorney and a son who is assistant chief at Chattanooga Fire Department. They also have two beautiful grandchildren.